Museum of Objects Burned by the Souls in Purgatory

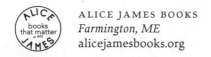

ALICE JAMES BOOKS
*Farmington, ME*
alicejamesbooks.org

# BURNED
# BY
# THE
# SOULS

POEMS

# MUSEUM

# OF

# OBJECTS

JEFFREY

THOMSON

# IN

# PURGATORY

10 9 8 7 6 5 4 3 2 1

Alice James Books are published by Alice James Poetry Cooperative, Inc.,
an affiliate of theUniversity of Maine at Farmington.

Alice James Books
114 Prescott Street
Farmington, ME 04938
www.alicejamesbooks.org

Library of Congress Cataloging-in-Publication Data

Names: Thomson, Jeffrey, author.
Title: Museum of objects burned by the souls in purgatory / Jeffrey Thomson.
Description: Farmington, ME : Alice James Books, 2022
Identifiers: LCCN 2021054811 (print) | LCCN 2021054812 (ebook)
    ISBN 9781948579254 (paperback) | ISBN 9781948579346 (epub)
Subjects: LCGFT: Poetry.
Classification: LCC PS3570.H6466 M87 2022  (print) | LCC PS3570.H6466 (ebook)
    DDC 811/.54—dc23
LC record available at https://lccn.loc.gov/2021054811
LC ebook record available at https://lccn.loc.gov/2021054812

Alice James Books gratefully acknowledges support from individual donors, private
foundations, the University of Maine at Farmington, the National Endowment for the
Arts, and the Amazon Literary Partnership. Funded in part by a grant from the Maine
Arts Commission, an independent state agency supported by the National Endowment
for the Arts.

Cover art: Tim Storrier, "The Grand Serendipity" 2016–2018 acrylic on canvas 200 x 300 cm

# TABLE OF CONTENTS

*for the ones we lost*

*The truth is out there*

—MULDER

# THE FOOT OF MARY MAGDALENE

*silver, glass, bone*

*in the church of San Giovanni Battista dei Fiorentini, Rome*

When they were set afloat
in a boat without sail or rudder
in the sea off of Galilee—
their lord dead, risen, and gone—
it wasn't a metaphor.

The sea shone hot and greasy
with summer. Fish perhaps
leapt up ladders of their own
bodies to climb into the mouths
of Magdalene, Lazarus still
stinking of death, and Martha,
her servant heart waiting
to be called.
           Some people say
they landed in Ephesus, that place
of mystery. Some people say
Magdalene landed in France
and lived thirty years in a cave.
Was fed bread and water
through the window by Martha
until her body became a box
of glass.

Or she was raised
into the sky by an angelic chorus
and fed the nectar of heaven
that tasted of certainty and stone.
Or she traveled to Rome and
brought an egg to Caesar
Tiberius. A red egg. Rebirth
and all that.
               But after her death
they divided her, these
same people, a tooth there,
a jawbone here, her arm
in London. Here in Rome,
the bones of her foot.
The reliquary elegant—
thin and silver-bronze
as scales, frozen and glamorous
as a fish made of dawn.
Such division was unsurprising,
really, the pieces of her spread
far and wide. Mary, she
had grown used to it.

But back in the boat,
their feet burning on the hot
staves, they are still wondering,
the three of them, where they will
land, what they will do without him.
The hot sun, the water, and still
the fish leap into their mouths
like answers to questions
they have not yet learned to ask.

# THE FINGERS OF
# DOUBTING THOMAS

*iron, glass, wood, bone*

*in the Basilica di Santa Croce in Gerusalemme, Rome*

what children's faces
he stroked with them
what fires intended or fruit
he plucked then peeled
and he dripping with nectar
what fish what bread
what olives what wine
what careless feeding

what dogs he scratched
their ears their hides
what cattle what cats
what donkeys what palms
their clattering fronds

what shit what piss
what wind what air
what seawater and sky
what blood what bruising
cut open to reveal what
what scars like white ropes
what hammers what nails

what women he's been inside
their mouths their cunts
what does he do wrong
what spices what dust
what dirt what doubt
what stone what death
what story what tongue
what gods he touched
what bodies what wounds

# THE TALE OF ST. PETER AND SIMON MAGUS

*volcanic basalt stone, iron bars*

*in the Basilica di Santa Francesca Romana, Rome*

The imprints of Peter's knees in the stone
tell a story: one with the Roman Forum

alive with magic, with the 1st century
and volcanic pavers in the street

square as the bell tower and
the basilica and Peter's name

which meant the rock
he became. He fell

to his knees as Simon soared into
the sky just the way the magician

boasted he could—the billow
of his robes a wild cacophony,

his beard a dark fire. This was an insult
to God. Peter couldn't let it slide

the way Simon slid above the pigeons
that chortled now below him.

Peter prayed with his arms
alight and wrenched Simon

from the clouds. Simon fell and broke
into parts and then the crowd stoned him

to death, which seems redundant. But,
Peter won, that's the message of the divots

worn in the stone here in the basilica.
Peter hauled Simon down with the ropes

of his prayers. It took some doing;
the force embedded Peter's knees

deep in the forum, after all. In the stone.
In the faith. But this story isn't

about that. It's about Simon.
Say what you want of him.

Say Simon was a charlatan.
Say Peter brought him down.

Say he broke into pieces. Whatever
you say—for a moment—Simon, he flew.

# ODE TO ELLA FITZGERALD AND
# THE BELVEDERE HERAKLES

*fragmentary marble statue in the Museo Pio Clementino*

Ella in Berlin *(live), February 13, 1960*

In Rome, late heat
along the theater

of Marcellus—
apartments above

grafted onto the bones
of the wrecked

body of the old world
and I'm listening

to Ella as she tries
"Mack the Knife"

in 1960 in Berlin,
in the rain

that smacks
the streets outside

the *Deutschlandhalle.*
The jilting lilt of the piano.

Damp scatter
of applause

as she begins
and quickly forgets

the lyrics. She charges into
the rafters of the song,

chasing fragments
she mangles

so perfectly, her voice
silk's idea of silk:

*What's the next chorus*
*to this song?*

*This is the one now*
*I don't know.*

Just as with
the Belvedere Herakles—

that half-a-statue,
thick trunk

of shattered
muscle—maybe

it's the heartbreak
of the broken,

simple wrongness
that makes everything

whole. Michelangelo
genuflected

before this statue,
before the muscle,

the bulwark,
and the broken junk

of the groin. He took
the image for St. Bartholomew

in his *Last Judgement,*
a man curled

over his own skin
and holding the knife

of martyrdom.
Across the river

the trees in Trastevere
shiver in the hot wind,

in the ragged ends
of the day

and Ella goes full growl.
She swings this

perfect wreck
of a song

the way Michelangelo
painted his own face

onto the empty envelope
of skin that was Bartholomew—

on the walls
of the Sistine Chapel.

The rest of Herakles
is gone, too,

but the torso remains,
that rocky stump of grace.

In Berlin, in the rain
gone gray, in the night,

the song ends. Here,
the lights come on

in the arcade,
on the bones

of the theater's tufa—
its skin of travertine

long gone.

# ST. BARTHOLOMEW FLAYED

*marble statue*

All Eyez on Me—*Tupac*

I am a man
with muscle
with veins
with my skin
peeled and
draped over
my own arm
like a Roman
cloak

I am a man
with faith
made visible
a man with
pain only
inside the
hollows of
his eyes I am
a man with
all eyes on
me on the
plinth on the
Duomo in
Milan

I    am    seen
I    am    seen
as   the   man
within a man
a        m a n
without fear
without
artifice
without
even
nakedness
to cover me

# HONCE LOUCOM |
# NEQUS VIOLATOD |
# NEQUE EXVEHITO

*lex spoletina—3rd century BC law stones, Spoleto, Italy*

*This sacred wood—inviolate—
no one shall cart or carry away
anything,* states the inscription
on the stone here where the hills
climb, where holm oaks hold
holly in their evergreen hands.
In this grove holy and ancient,
the stone lays out the rules: *No
one must cut wood in it—except on
the day worship takes place.*

These trees hold hush, thought
Francis in the 13th century. On
the forest floor, he walked. He
spoke with swallows. He asked
for silence. To his monks, he
spoke control. He crept inside
a cold cell carved into the
limestone cliff here to sleep in a
silence older than the trees. He
slept with a hand to his chest.

He knew the rules. He made the rules. His heaven was built from the lumber of denial. He slept for a long time in the quiet acre of that certainty.

Then in 1798, Napoleon's soldiers hauled into the air here their own tree in the sacred wood, a tree of liberty, of celebration. They were honoring the storming of the Bastille, after all. They lit a pyre, they reveled with eyes full of freedom and comrades long gone. They raised a glass and their hands. They sang, they drank, they shat. They profaned the sacred wood with raucous women.

*In this grove let no one perform sacrifices for dead relations.*

In their liberty—beneath this new tree they built—they thought they were free from the past. Thought they held fate in their hands the way they held the breasts of women who knelt above them in the holy grove.

*If anyone shall have acted contrary to*
*this let there be a judgment rendered.*

Please forgive them. They reveled
and were happy. Forgive them,
please. They just didn't know
the rules.

# FOUND EGYPTIAN LOVE POTION SONNET

*ink on papyrus*

Take dandruff from the scalp
of a dead man murdered
and seven grains of barley
buried in the grave of a child
and crush with ten apple pips.
Add the blood of a tick
from a black dog, a drop
of blood from the ring finger
of your left hand, and your semen.
Grind acacia seeds with honey,
add to the mix beneath Khonsu's
house of night. Should this not work,
rub your phallus with the foam
of the mouth of a stallion instead.

# THE TALE OF THE GREAT MARTYR
# DEMETRIUS, THE MYRRH-GUSHER

*silk, bone, myrrh*

I had to write this for the name
alone, for the sexual hovering

not even below the surface,
for Demetrius whose bones

are in Pittsburgh, for Demetrius
whose story is Roman, is proconsul

in Thessaloniki. He was a closeted
Christian, of course, who confessed

something to Emperor Maximian—
that name like a sexual position.

For Demetrius who was locked away
in a bathhouse while Maximian watched

his champion galivant around the circus.
That guy was a Vandal, yes, like those who come

in the night, and he got pincushioned
on a bed of upturned spears. It's phalluses

all the way down in this one,
my friends. I am writing this

for Demetrius who was run through
with spears, too, and the homoerotic.

I am writing this for lost love,
for the holy moment of orgasm,

for the arch of the back,
for the hips, for the whole body

of the boy who kissed me on
the mouth at that party

in the basement of nowhere special
in Pittsburgh. *I just couldn't help it,*

he said. I am writing this for his
bravery not mine because

that was years ago and he's dead
now. I writing this because

he confessed something
in that moment, a hidden faith

that puzzles me still. He put *desire*
on the end of a spear and offered it

to me, handle first. I am writing this
for desire, for Demetrius, I mean,

for his bones. They were meant for
the dogs. They were buried in secret.

They weep myrrh, it is said,
gush it to this day, wrapped in silk

in some basement in Pittsburgh.

# HAN SOLO IN CARBONITE

*I will not give up my favorite decoration*

—JABBA

he adorns the wall in the
palace with a small regalia
of dials and knobs is well-
lit gallery style is elegant is
tasteful he has found a small
peaceful alcove of his own
heroism to hang in a beautiful
stasis that lies opposite the
gore and tilt of his everyday
life for he has run every day
from the empire of his own
choices his whole legend a
version of the word *escape*
we have all watched so many
times we know the story by
heart so when he walks into
that contraption at the end
of the film the descent into
flashing lights and smoke into
technology and Chewbacca
howling we see it is his last
free step even though he
will escape the carbonite
and return he is still in this

moment in this moment he is
art in a lonely lovely alcove of
a desert palace

# ODE TO MY STERNUM

*after cardiac surgery*

o bulwark o damaged
palisade o broken
Roman shield that
guards yet the ferocious
snail of my still beating
heart that aging sack
of thud and muscle
o broken latch to a
box of lightning box of
magic o struck oak still
smoldering with white
fire o breached wall o
ruin o cleft in the rock
filled in with quartz
o sore and battered
chest that aches now
when the cold comes
off the ocean in fall and
leaves muck the gutters
with their bodies and
clog the sewer until
finally the rain comes
and the pressure builds
and the small dam is
cleared away and the
water moves once more

# TWO HALVES OF THE SKULL
# OF JOHN THE BAPTIST

*transparent crystal, sections of a human head, silver plate*

*in the Amiens Cathedral, France, and the Basilica di San Silvestro in Capite, Rome*

he was not the one

          *Salome wanted*

he wore

          *his head*

a goat's skin

          *she was the one*

not the one

          *who cried*

John

          *in her wilderness*

he lived in

          *of palace*

a wild desert

          *and moon*

he was the coming of

          *there is always*

the light

          *another*

light shone

          *she was the one*

in his face

          *who took his head*

he called the dove

*she looked*

down

*upon his head*

he was not the one

*shoulder bare*

who walked

*bright*

into a Jerusalem

*the silver platter*

paved with palms

*spun with*

there is always

*moonlight*

another

# FOUND SONNET IN
# LINES FROM PLINY

*Natural History: 28.98-99*

A woman is guaranteed to carry
a pregnancy to term if she wears
around her neck the white flesh
from a hyena's chest with seven
of its hairs and a stag's genitals
tied up in the leather of a gazelle.

A hyena's genitals, consumed
with honey, increases desire
for sex, even if men— typically—
despise sex with women. Really,
the peace of the whole home
relies upon keeping these genitals
and a spine with the skin still on it
close at hand.

# THE TALE OF THE WELL OF MARY

*in Santa Maria in Via, Rome*

*the year of our Lord, 1256*

It's the horses
stabled behind
the church
that one night
in early September
I think of,
an ordinary night
full of dark
and small fires,
full of rest
for tired they were,
for content
and brushed down
they were
and busy with
their oats
but spent from
the day's labor
crossing
the glamour
of Italy
that even then
shone gossamer

and gold
in the evening's
ending hour.

When the servant
of Cardinal Capocci
dropped a tile
with the blessed
Madonna blessedly
painted on it
into the nearly
dry well
in their stall,
of course
the water rose
and kept on rising.
Water came up
and up from
the earth,
forever and
ever, amen.
It over-
flowed the basin,
filled the stalls
like faith itself.
Unlike that night
in Bethlehem
when the golden
light of the eternal
word was made
into time
and bounded

around the stable,
filling every animal
in the manger
with a language
like water,
they had nothing
to say,
these horses.
They snorted.
They stamped.
They rolled
their eyes white.
They called out
fear with the full
weight of their bodies.
They wanted nothing
to do with this
lady of the waters,
lady of the overflow,
lady of perpetual
milk and honey.
They wanted silence
and rest, amen,
wanted food
and sleep,
but they were
commanded
to receive the
terrifying miracle
of abundance
and a blessing
everlasting,

a liquid forever
that shone on
and on and never
ended—*never*—
not even
in a small dark
stall full of rest
and oats and
sleep trundling
on into the night.

# THE TALE OF THE GRIEF STOPPER

*A stone created by this river is called the pausilypos. Anyone grieving*
*who finds this stone is immediately relieved of the pain that holds him.*

—PSEUDO-PLUTARCH

On the day another boy
was shot, I took a stone
from this river. On the day
I heard his name, I lifted it.
I held it. It glittered
in the summer sun.
Aspens fluttered.
Cicadas thrummed.
I caressed its small, soft
skull. The boy was six
years old. He was
at a garlic festival
when he was shot.
Greeks placed bulbs
of garlic on cairns
at crossroads—a gift
for Hecate—as protection
from demons.

It was the son of Poseidon
who threw himself
into this river, it is said,
when his own son marched
against his neighbors

and was killed. He was
held down by water,
by the water's hands
which are not hands
the way water is not grief.
His grief turned the river.
Now all we have are stones.
They are hard and small
like something in my shoe.
Like someone is walking
on my soul. He was six
years old. The river
is dry now.
The water is gone.
Aspens quake
in the bright air.
Cicadas crackle.
All that's left
are stones.

# CAUSE AND EFFECT

*in the holy grove, the Sanctuary of Monteluco, Spoleto*

Because five small cells
of the convent survive
and their doors rise
only to my shoulder,
because planks
and wooden pillows,
because pain
is a dutiful tutor,
because a shelf
and an urn
for water, because
simplicity is the sign
of faith and water
is its symbol.
Because tears.
Because Francis
demanded poverty,
after all, because once
when ill he ate chicken—
just bone-broth
scented with sage
from a hillside
of cypress and clover—
to recover his strength;
he shamed himself
so thoroughly that

as he entered Assisi
he demanded
his brother rope
his neck and drag him
through the gate,
shouting, *Come,*
*look at the glutton*
*who has been fattening*
*on poultry when you did not*
*know it.* Because many
flocked to see
so strange a sight,
because they wept
together and heaved
repeated sighs.

They wept for
their pain,
which is the same
as all of ours,
after all, because
they wept not
for Francis in his chapel,
threadbare Francis
who spoke to the birds
on this hillside,
in this grove of holm
oaks. Because here
in this church
coil the chains
he scoured across
his back, washing

himself clean of craving,
because here
the rock is carved
where he retreated
to hide his soul
from the world.

They surely wept
for their own souls
that wander lost
among the oaks,
for their thirsts
that cannot be sated,
because Francis
released water
from the rock
to chase away
the thirst of his brothers:
tiny men with wooden
clogs and bodies
made of scars.
Because it flows still—
this thin coil
of water in the convent
beside the tiny cells,
the rough beds,
and austerity—
and their wounds
are like ours,
after all, what
they hold onto
most dearly.

# SACRO CORPORALE,
# OR THE MIRACLE AT BOLSENA

*lineń altar cloth, blood, silver, glass*

*in the Duomo di Orvieto*

in the year of our Lord / 1263 / Peter of Prague /
walked away / he walked a long way / away / he
walked over / hills he walked through / chestnut
forests / along the way / the sun opened them / into
small cathedrals / he walked through / Bohemia he
walked / to Rome / he walked / over the world / he
doubted / the miracle doubting / as he walked / he
could not / believe the bread / became / the body
the wine / became / blood he walked / because he
believed / he had been called / by lack of faith / he
had been / summoned / he walked to Rome / Rome
was not enough / he walked home / he stopped
walking / at this ancient / even then / church in
Bolsena / he stopped / as a way / to celebrate mass /
he walked to the altar / he raised / the host aloft / in
the air / of his disbelief / he blessed it / with doubt /
he tore the bread / it bled / across his hands / across
the linen altar cloth / he tried to hide / the blood / the
bread bled / the body bled / it stained his hands / the
floor / he walked away / it stained / the whole world

# FOUND SONNET ON THE RECIPE

# FOR THE PHILOSOPHER'S STONE

*translated from the English*

*in the Dante Museum, Florence*

Dissolve the bodies of your enemies in water.
Do what I say. You who want the sun or moon
alive as fire inside you, dissolve those bodies
in water and give that water to your friend
to drink, you know the one. Give him nothing
to eat. When he has died, you will see him
covered in black fur like the young leopard
inside the body of an old lion. Bury him—
*do it!* I say—until his bones, muscles, and joints
dissolve and turn to water. From that water
obtain earth. The stone will be there and more:
something that multiplies. It is simple: from earth
obtain water, from water stone. Practice this
and become master of what subjugates us all.

# THE TALE OF THE HOLY FORESKIN:

# CALCATA VECCHIA, ITALY

*the uncircumcised child whose flesh of his foreskin*
*is not circumcised that soul shall be cut off from his people*
—GENESIS 17:14

this one is missing
the flesh of Jesus
the blood lost
for us
for the first time
I held my son
down
on the exam table
small warble
of his pain
a bird in the river
birch outside
as the knife
lifted a piece
of him
in the manger Mary
held this piece of
her son
listened to his wails
to the thin
cries of angels
hovering above

the stable
like terrible birds
the moment
was calm
was bright
the doctor's office
filled with September
sunlight
the wine grapes
ripening in the fields
magpies in the river birch
it was taken from Mary
in mystery
by a woman who
was likely
an angel in disguise
was carted off
was sealed
and stored
in oil
in Jerusalem
the doctor lifted the skin
of my son smeared
with his blood
as I had asked
I held him down
I held him still
then came Charlemagne
his crusade his soldiers
like small knives
he has no memory
of this

he has no memory
of this specific pain

the soldiers brought
it to Italy
to a town on a tip
of volcanic tufa
the bare church tower
looming quiet and simple
this piece of Jesus
was saved was kept
in glass in gold
in a cup like a crown
in a head of crystal
held aloft by angels
always angels
and in 1983
the flesh of Jesus
disappeared
for the last time
stolen again
from those
who wanted
it most

his flesh is lost
I held him down
magpies lifted off
the tree outside
the window
they vanished
the way pieces of us

always do
he has no memory
of the church
tower bare
shorn of ornament
birch trees
empty in autumn
the moment bright
the moment calm
in the manger

# MUSEUM OF OBJECTS BURNED
# BY THE SOULS IN PURGATORY

*various objects*

*in the Chiesa del Sacro Cuore del Suffragio, Rome*

the way
the prayer book
the text has faded
the way the ashes
of the book
or the way
the wooden table
and chemise
a burned hand
the skeletal clutching
char marks
ghosted only
in a tiny bedchamber
filled with
this small language
all these objects say
*say something please*

a burnt hand touches
the way
five burned fingers
caress the opened page
*The Imitation of Christ*
they stroke
lift the sleeve
of the venerable Mother Isabella Fornari
paws at her
the nightshirt of Joseph Leleux
on a 500 Lira note
at its edges
a museum
all this eros
this love
something
about desire

# THE TALE OF THE UNCORRUPTED BODY OF ST. SEBASTIAN OF THE CARTS

*human body, silver, glass*

*in el Templo Conventual de San Francisco, Puebla, México*

Sebastian was told not to
give his cloak away—he was

constantly giving things
away: his last loaf of bread,

a head of lettuce wet with dew,
the final kindness of his plate,

and the abbot was sick of it.
Sebastian agreed, you see,

but he told the beggar he found
on the road covered

as that man was in a wealth
of his own piss and pinhole scabs

that he could not stop him
from taking the cloak by force.

So, the beggar did. It was his way,
Sebastian, I mean. In his youth,

a plague had come for him
and his village in Spain.

He alone survived.
A wolf came out of the hills

and took from him the tumor
that grew inside his gullet

like a vein of liquid
gold, like a sign

of what was to come.
The wolf burst the tumor

like a bladder of bad wine,
lapped the pus, covered

himself with it. He gave it
freely, Sebastian did, to the wolf.

It was his generosity
that mattered, you see.

Even in death, Sebastian held his body
close, kept it fresh, for who knew

when it might be needed
again. They kept checking,

the abbot and his minions,
I mean, in the temple

of San Francisco. His body
was waiting. It stayed soft,

incorruptible as gold.
A hundred and twenty years

later he was ready
when revolution burst

into Mexico. When soldiers
tried to lap up the wealth

of the church, they opened
the walls and filled them

with holes.
They plundered, they perforated,

and finding nothing took
a dagger and opened

the body of Sebastian
looking for his golden heart.

Sebastian was ready.
He gave them his insides

the way he gave his tumor
to the wolf. He bathed them

in his bowels, blessed them,
I mean, with all that richness.

# FOUND POEM WITH JOHN POCH'S LIST OF FORBIDDEN WORDS FOR POEMS

| | |
|---|---|
| Scream | if you must, but this isn't |
| Pain | nor is it the |
| Soul | with its own rough |
| Beauty | like the oyster shell of a |
| Dream | (so sleek on the inside, so sassy) where |
| Tears | become |
| Thoughts | and weld themselves to |
| Desire | in the |
| Heart | of this nacreous |
| Life | and a strange |
| Feeling | that |
| Hope | has |
| Forever | abandoned us to |
| Hate | with its metal arms, |
| Fear | with its treadmill. It isn't |
| Emotion | (what kind, you ask?), not |
| Dark | |
| Passion | that tastes of high tide, nor the |
| Love | of |
| Death | or |
| Sweet | |
| Depression | with its buttery |
| Warmth | but this poem is a little |
| Sad, | honestly, with the |

| | |
|---|---|
| Stress | of so many late nights filtering the saltwater of the |
| Spirit | all the while seabirds |
| Cry | their |
| Grief | in a chittering |
| Song, | cut the sky to pieces, and |
| Embrace | the |
| Perfect | |
| Aspirations | of their kind. All this poem asks is that you |
| Engulf | that sadness. |
| Caress | the grit of your |
| Memory | until it produces a |
| Vision | solid and glossy as a pearl. Then |
| Sit | and |
| Stare | at it until each word becomes unbearably yours. |

# HOW IT BEGAN

*King who devours his people*
—THE ILIAD, *Book I*

Beneath the rain of Apollo's
plague arrows, Agamemnon
cried out, *We have it totally*
*under control. It's going*
*to be just fine.* First,
Apollo went for the mules—
the weeping sacks of their bodies
and the dogs who orbited
the camp like a loose constellation
of thin stars in the eastern sky
when the sun has just set—
before cutting down the men.
*You have 15 people, and*
*the 15 within a couple*
*of days is going to be down*
*to close to zero,* Agamemnon
said. It came on like
the gathering of dark
along the edges of the trees
when dusk walks across
the land, her dark cloak
spreading, and beyond
the great walls of Troy
stand high and still visible
in the failing of the day

and the corpse fires burn
day and night, no end in sight.
*It's going to disappear,* he said.
*It's like a miracle. It will disappear.*

# POEM WITH THE NAME OF
# A COSTA RICAN BEACH

*Sal si Puedes, Osa Peninsula*

yes it means
brown pelicans
chop the surf
for fish yes
scarlet macaws
chase shadows
across olive sand
the sky stunned
blue and black
hawks hunt
what the water
tosses out yes
but when the tide
turns it means
there is
no way out
when the surf
against the cliff
thrashes the shore
in the heat
in the night
in the tent
when the surf
pauses when

the sound
hesitates the silence
startles as if yes
the one sleeping
next to you
has suddenly
yes suddenly
stopped
breathing

# FOUND POEM FOR THE FIRST APRIL OF THE PANDEMIC

*golden shovel sonnet for Samuel L. Jackson and T. S. Eliot*

In the airport parking lot with ice shelving off the cars, I
want to wake to a dream of summer blazed with *have*
and hot blossom, an orchestra of insect sex cascading. I had
hope once. It melted into the bodies of those I loved. It
felt like wind ceasing—the way that silence starts with
stilled breath, startles in my imagined gardens of aloe and these
magenta torches of wild ginger. All this is hard on you, mother-
to-my-child; you hold onto things the way the scent of fucking
lingers in damp earth. The smell of the body that snakes
through ferns coiled and unfiddled in the resting beds on
the edge of the yard. We are the corpse in Eliot's garden, this
unripe fruit of a body blooming and abandoned. Oh, mother-
to-the-future, we are long gone from that fucking
paradise and hope grows distant as a departing plane.

# SKULL OF A YOUNG TIGHTROPE WALKER WHO DIED OF A BROKEN NECK, 1934

*human skull, glass*

*in the Mütter Museum, Philadelphia*

I am more
than those
last seconds
wobble and
then the
evaporation
of hope I
was once
grace on a
wire once
elegance
and perfect
wonder
you see
almost
falling is
harder than
not anyone
can walk a
wire only

the best can
pretend to
fall     for
nothing's
easier than
failure
there's
a quick grip
on the stale
absence
of the air
then    the
ground
living is hard
hard is an
only  child
making
a pietà
in     his
mother's
arms hard is
a    mother
walking
away

# HAUNTED ODE ON
# EL DÍA DE LOS MUERTOS

*marigold petals, black & white photograph, wooden crates*

*in the public market, Puebla, México*

Odysseus used the long edge
of his sword to slit the throats
of sheep at the gates of Hades
and blood spilled and wrapped
his feet in new sandals of crimson.
The ghosts of his past lined up
to lap the gore. They stood
with serenity, with need
practiced long and constant.
They wailed their patience
silently and fierce, demanded
a taste, to bathe even the tips
of their tongues in the bruised
nothing left of an animal's life.

But, here in Puebla, when autumn
creeps down the throat of México
and the spume of the volcano
rises like a ghost above the town,
the spirit of Pedro Infante
lingers above the marigolds
and packing crates of his *offerta*.

He hovers above shredded
petals, a wave of gold stones
in the market glowing with the sun
and the results of a late rain.
His headshot, black-and-white and still
flirtatious, still with that glint
in his eye. He wants to sing
again. He knows what
the lonely wives of México want:
to hear the songs of love
he crooned. Their notes linger

in the air the way Achilles hovered
beyond the grasp of Odysseus
saying, *Let me taste it, let me*
*taste my life just once more.*
Women turn on the radio
again. They want to hear him
one more time, to feel
that burning of the skin
the weak-kneed rush
in the loins. Their husbands
snore in their chairs and
the women they sharpen
long knives in the kitchen.
Outside the window,
ficus leaves silver as ghosts
flutter down the wet street.

# HUNGER STONES

*carved boulders, river*

*in the Czech town of Děčín*

when I was dying
along the Elbe
grass sere as thirst
and the beeches
burnt to bone
by sun and heat
the days so dry
the sky felt
like fired clay
I took the time
to carve
*If you see me, weep*
onto a table
of stone revealed
by the retreating
water of the dying
river the sky burned
as I worked
as it burns now
and forever amen
I exhausted myself
there but it was
necessary you see

I needed to tell
someone but you
you misunderstand
I did not do it
for me
I did it for you

# HOW IT BURNED

In the photo of Notre Dame, three ravens swim in the churn of smoke and flame.

Ravens live close to the end of the world in our stories. They are hungry and the cathedral is consumed. They are ready. They like it this way.

On that façade, one can see the carving of St. Denis, patron Saint of France.

In French, ravens are sometimes called *prêtre,* or priest.

Yes, that is his own head that he's holding.

*Prêtre* comes from the Greek—πρεσβύτερος, *presbuteros*—meaning on old man, an elder. Despite the fact that the Greek appears to use the term *eros*, the word does not derive from desire.

When the Romans cut his head from his body near where *Monmartre* now stands, his dark hair looked like a nest for ravens, it was said.

Ravens mimic the calls of other species; they even imitate human words.

He picked it up. He walked miles through poplars fruited with ravens mocking him, calling out his name. He walked as far as he could.

They sometimes wait in trees as ewes give birth, then attack the newborn lambs.

This, too, is part of the story.

*Prêtre habitué* means *to be in the habit of*. In the colloquial it means: *Get used to it.*

Baudelaire: *Il n'existe que trois êtres respectables; le prêtre, le guerrier, le poète. Savoir, tuer, et créer.*

He collapsed.

Young ravens are fond of playing games with sticks, repeatedly dropping them then diving to catch them in midair.

He carried his head like knowledge, like a comrade, like a small dark bundle of faith as long as he could.

The priest, the soldier, the poet.

When his head finally fell from his hands, ravens left the trees. They returned with pieces of wood, as if to preparing to build something.

*Savoir, tuer, et créer.* To know, to kill, and to create.

From the trees they called out a sound that might have been *prêtre* or may have been *prêtre habitué*. It is hard to be sure.

# MUSA UNDERWATER
# SCULPTURE GARDEN

*concrete, coral, sea fans*

*below Isla Mujeres, México*

here the sea is the color of glass clear
and green and azure and sunlight
heats the sky spangles the waves
just a few miles off the Yucatan here
the rising tide tears away at the
foundations of the hotels the sea
walls the breakwaters eats away at
the footings pulls the earth out to a
sea as unrelenting as the sun

here too beneath the water my
body's weight is weightless beneath
the water there are stone bodies
heavier than my body's weight
beneath the water like those Chinese
soldiers standing forever buried in a
hill famed for jade and gold buried
with palaces with towers with rivers
made of mercury buried beneath
the stars of an artificial sky buried
by the god-emperor who wanted

his world to go on and on forever
without end

here these bodies wait eyeless
and grow coral grow sea fans here
beneath the water they raise their
faces and pray to their sky that is
first water and then a silver shelf of
air beneath the water they wait and
with them in this water clear as the
wings of angels triggerfish nimble as
fingers and needlefish little slices of
light the color of the sky at dawn

beneath the water these bodies wait
beneath this water that is the color
of heat rising all over the land water
the color of the eyes of a God who
buries us beneath this sky here above
the Yucatán here above a world we
want to last forever and ever amen

# ODE TO *LE GRAND K*

*International Prototype Kilogram developed after the*
*French Revolution and stored in Saint-Cloud, Paris*

o you were once pure water
you were once a liter
you were once Greek
words meaning one
thousand small weights
o portion o quantity
you were once
platinum-iridium
a cylinder with edges
at a four-angle to minimize
wear you were once
the monarch of measure
stored in glory on a small
throne of double glass bells

but regal purity is never
enough loss is built in
to every object and you
were diminished you
were deficient
you were lack and
even so little loss
was too much
so we turned to
the weightless flame

of pure math and
anchored the kilogram
in Planck's constant

now *Grand K* you are
obsolete antediluvian
just a lector reading Flaubert
to rooms of men rolling
cigars thick as thumbs
or a lamplighter carrying
paraffin and a box of
a thousand small fires
that rise up in the night
and burn even the king

# ODE TO THE STONE SPHERES

*gabbro spheres*

*in the Diquís Delta, Costa Rica*

this is for the ones we don't
understand      why they
punctuate muddled fields of
banana      dot colonnades of
oil palm   huge stones   basalt
and perfect      gray as minds
in the green mist of these
pineapple          plantations
gray as grease      in Palma Sur

there is so much ignorance
the why        of them the
who   because dead because
the Spanish because their
own pandemic  and the how
of them   because   they
are      so          round   so
perfect       because  in  the
1930s when workers cleared
the rain forest they found
these stones spheres   perfect
as our planet   they pushed
them              aside with
bulldozers  with horsepower

inspired by stories of hidden
gold   workmen drilled them
blew them open with craving
with dynamite

the pieces fell apart their
centers did not hold anything
we have broken the world we
have the remains  they are all
around us    we do not
understand why    they do
not    fit back together

# THE TALE OF THE ALPHABET

begins with the marriage of the daughter of love and war. Her name is Harmony. Cadmus is her bridegroom. The tables are strong with candles. Their lights look like blades in the dark. The meat is crisp with pepper and olives. Dates and plums and pomegranates glisten. Harmony is the daughter of love and war. Cadmus is a man. A hero. He was meant to fight the warriors who grew from the dragon's teeth but he was clever and threw a rock among them and they turned on themselves in self-slaughter. His parents are there—proud and shining like lanterns. An old uncle, crusty as a wolf. Some villagers. The local butcher. A childhood friend.

The gods—her relatives—the gods are at this meal, too. Aphrodite glowing. Ares, coarse and wearing the skins of men. Zeus and Hera have stopped fighting for the night. Apollo stands off to one side, regal as a knife. The tables blush with abundance. There is the chatter the gods favor. The stories. There is laughter, laughter, laughter. There is feasting, there is song. The couple is happy. Her name is Harmony. Everything is bright.

There are stories in the night, stories of heroes, of monsters. Long rambling stories that echo and repeat. There are many gifts, including a necklace that brings misfortune to whoever wears it. This is the essential condition of the gifts of the gods, but no one recognizes that, yet.

When the night is nearly over, the gods have one last present for the couple: the alphabet. The couple doesn't know quite what to do with this strange accumulation of stick and sound, but they are grateful. It is a gift from the gods, after all.

They take the alphabet and the gods retire. Nothing is ever the same. This is the last time the gods sit down with men. Something changes this night, but no one knows that yet, either.

Harmony and Cadmus begin to write things down. They are hesitant, at first. They work at a long table. The night outside the window billows and is deep. They don't quite know how to make this household of shapes work. The stories on the page do not match the stories in their heads. But they persist. It becomes a little easier. The sun rises. It sets. The days smell of pine and hot stone. At first words and then sentences. Easier and easier each day. Sentences like strings. Now they're writing all the stories down. Fixing them in place. Stories of love. Stories of war. Stories of heroes and monsters and gods. Sometimes it is hard to tell them apart. Stories with sentences that stretch for miles like fences. They write and the past is fixed behind them. They write and the gods are finally kept at bay.

# INFINITE JEST

*wrought iron grill, glass, gold*

*in the basilica Parrocchiale San Lorenzo in Lucina, Rome*

Lorenzo was mortar for the church
he built. He gathered wild birds
for the rafters and fruited trees
for their food. He carted stone
and hoisted, he pestled, he block-
and-tackled. Persecuted
by Valerian and about to be
arrested, Lorenzo goatherded
the church's wealth, distributed it
to the poor. He paid the unmade
orphans, clothed the lepers
in money. He sold the sacred
vessels, the varied trestles.
He chased out the birds—
all to increase his offering
to the world. Valerian demanded
Lorenzo deliver the money
and so Lorenzo pointed to
the lepers and said,
*This the treasure of the church.*
For this jape he was immediately
seized and was released from
holding on to some of his blood.
For this he was grilled alive

on the steps of the temple.
He called out halfway through,
*It is well done, turn me over.*
For that jest he became
the patron saint of comedians,
but what's really funny is that
no one mentions what Valerian—
some sorry heckler on a throne
of gold—said in return.
The story finishes in the grill
marks across his chest
like rafters of pain holding him
aloft. No one mentions
the absolute end when
Lorenzo's head left
his shoulders with a snicker
of the blade and the birds
chortled away into a sky
fraught with distant clouds.

# TWO SHEEP GOD

Five thousand years ago in Sumer, the words *two sheep god Inanna* were scored into a clay tablet with a reed stylus.

They are first written words we know of.

They are either a receipt or they are a story.

*God.* Inanna is the goddess of sex and war and justice.

We can see the thinking as it begins. The power and potential of the sentence.

Inanna carries the sky and wears the sun in her hair. She climbed down into *Kur*—the underworld—but failed to conquer it and was killed.

*Two.* The doubleness of the word. The more than one.

Her beloved consort is Dumuzid, the shepherd. He is rangy and wild. His hair is a tangle of knots and bees. His is the vigor that causes sap to rise in trees, but he is mostly a thin seedling, without muscle.

*Sheep.* The category. The object.

Very few prayers are addressed to him, and most are requests for milk, more grain, a few more sheep.

The sacrifice Inanna favored was sheep. They were Dumuzid's charge—his responsibility. She demanded what he most loved.

It is this way: *I, a humble shepherd, offer two sheep to Inanna.*

Following her, Dumuzid laddered down into hell; he tried so hard to rescue her.

Or it is this: *I, Inanna, accept your offering.*

This sentence is both a receipt and a thought. Inanna is both the subject and the object of devotion.

There is so much lost.

*Two sheep god Inanna.*

But that's not what it says. It's in the passive voice.

Someone gave two sheep to the temple. We don't know who.

Dumuzid failed and he was punished. The sentence requires that he spend half of every year in the land of the dead.

The price was paid.

# GALILEO'S MIDDLE FINGER
# OR *E PUR SI MUOVE*

*human tissue and glass in the Museo Galileo, Florence*

Under house arrest in his villa—
the golden smoke of Florence
fencing him in—he is forced
to read the seven
penitential psalms once a day
for three years. *Blessed*
*are they whose iniquities*
*are forgiven,* he reads.

He thinks about tides
sloshing the seas across
the world. He thinks about
comets and how
they move. He thinks
about circles that forever
return, about his father,
a lutenist long dead,
who discovered that
on a stretched string
the pitch varies as
the square root
of the tension. Pressure
of his life taut, he is
that string, he is certain.

He knows Bruno
was hung upside down
naked and wreathed
in fire and smoke
in the *Campo de' Fiori*
for thoughts like these.
Escaped that fate he has.
He will live his life
in this villa until
his eyes fail and his sleep.
He keeps reading.
His middle finger traces
the path of the words.
The evening spins
around him across a sky
frozen with stars.

# THE HEART OF ST. LAURENCE O'TOOLE

*human cardiac tissue, iron*

*in Christ Church Cathedral, Dublin*

everyone trusted him
in Ireland
in 1166
the Vikings
the Irish
all glistening
and hard
as beaks
in their armor
in their ferocity
in their beards
of smolder and rage
during the invasion
the Norman invasion
he walked among them
armed only
with his heart
he stopped a massacre
but it's never enough
peace never lasts
in Dublin
on streets pooled

with black water
with the shit of horses
and men
wet slaughter
all that dying
his own house cluttered
with refugees
with weeping
he walked among
warriors among thieves
he told them to trust him
his voice a bird
some raptor perhaps
calling to them all
from the hawthorn
*stop* he told them
and they did
*all will be well* he said
and for a short while
it was centuries
later when
the small wrinkled bird
of his heart
was stolen
from its cage
thieves took it
poor and foolish
they thought
it would save them
but the heart
although
it returned

and reassured everyone
the way he always did
was never going to be
enough peace
never lasts
the heart
killed their families
with small wickedness
with heart attacks
with its song
they said they heard it
calling
in their dreams
in the streets
as they walked
it called like a raptor
in a cage
demanding
to be let free
beyond the gray
bars of the sky

# HOW WE SURVIVED

*We locked the doors and let nobody in*
—ELLEN BRYANT VOIGHT, *Kyrie*

The virus began in an animal, perhaps a bat.

We spoke to each other in the small mirrors of our phones.

We locked the doors. We let nobody in.

By this time, the Achaean army had been camped on the beach outside the walls of Troy for ten years.

The virus contains spike proteins, armatures that it uses to grab and penetrate the outer walls of cells.

We baked a small acreage of bread. We built palisades of wine bottles.

The Trojan walls were built by Poseidon. It was said they could never be breached by an enemy.

The spike protein has a grappling hook that grips onto host cells and a cleavage site—a molecular can opener that allows the virus to crack open and enter.

We locked the doors. We let nobody in.

Calchas, the seer, knew the past and the future. He knew why and what was to come.

It starts with a fever, a dry cough, and then, later, shortness of breath.

Achilles asked Calchas for help—he asked, *Why?* but not *What is to come?* No one wants to know that.

Our body senses a foreign invader.

We distanced ourselves like fields of grass. We quarried isolation.

The Greeks—you know this part—built an enormous horse and filled it with their bodies, filled it with their ten-year rage.

Fluid builds in the lungs as the virus replicates and breaks open more and more cells.

The Trojans took the horse inside their city.

Fever. Difficulty breathing.

We built walls. High walls. We thought they were unbreachable.

Multi-organ failure, respiratory failure, septic shock.

The horse unbuckled itself in the dark. The Achaeans flowed out with their fires and their swords.

# MEMENTO MORI

*a late Gothic period funerary monument*

*in the Church of Saint-Étienne, France*

René de Chalon you were a prince
in *Bar-le-Duc* you were the last
prince of Orange you were so
young you ate the tongues of swan
of peacock drank spiced wine
fermented pomegranate nectar you
danced the farandole the pavane
you were so young you died at
twenty-five in the siege of Saint-
Dizier as Charles the Fifth advanced
into Champagne a campaign that
sounds more pleasant than it was
René de Chalon you were shot you
died with the Emperor by your side
and your lands went to your cousin
William the Silent who had nothing
to say you were so young your wife
in memorial called not your name
again and again in her sleep but for
a life-sized statue not heroic not
mounted atop a charger rearing
not stoic in defeat instead she had
carved from limestone          this
putrefying skeleton with strips of

dried skin flapping over a hollow
carcass she wanted to say all is
transient all must fail but if I say
I am sorry      if I say memory is
the black marble columns that hold
your funeral drapery if I say life is
often not as pleasant as it sounds if
I call you into being here again you
might  only  point to your empty
ribcage because your wife placed
the shriveled plum of your true
heart in your hand now your heart
is gone René you were so young it
was stolen during the Revolution
in its place rests only an oval stone
smooth as the sound of your name

# THE WELL OF THE STAFF

*stone, seawater, swans*

*just north of Sligo, Ireland*

Here Patrick opened a lesser
hole in the rock, not
the holy pool at Clonmel
where the faithful bathe
whole-bodied to slather
on the miraculous, nor
the well of shaving where
he and his companions,
old men, all, left their beards
behind and climbed into robes
of youth. This well is small
and sorry by the edge
of the sea where swans
like the nine-and-fifty
Yeats wrote of gather
at the outflow of the Abbey,
so downriver my son
and I walk along the lane
and through the gate
to the hole in the rocky shore,
to the well with its water
green with algae and weed
and a cup for drinking—

*Kneel and Pray* chipped
into the stone before it.

I am old and he is young
and what I would pray for
is small and sorry as well
and mocked by the cirrus
sky. Still there is magic
in the world, so fifteen pebbles
we gather and five circles
we make. Three sips of water
we take: one for the father,
one for the son, one for
the holy ghost who flutters
in the hawthorn tree
in strips of cloth, old earbuds,
worn rosaries. All the tangled
detritus of belief left hanging
in the wind because
here the old world hangs on
and becomes young again,
here swans spool their legs
in the bay waiting,
as Yeats said, to scatter
wheeling in great broken rings.

# THE TALE OF THE *TITUS CRUCIS*

*carved wooden tablet written in Hebrew, Greek, and Latin*

*in the Basilica di Santa Croce in Gerusalemme, Rome*

Helena is busy / in this year of our lord  / 325 / she has
traveled / to Jerusalem / wants to bring back gifts / for her
son / Constantine / for an emperor / for example / in a shop
/ in a church / she finds a silver-gilt / casket some nails / a
piece of wood / old wood / carved wood / *Iesus Nazarenus*/
*Rex Iudaeorum* / INRI / wood with words / that will be /
painted in / a thousand frescos / carved / into millions / of
hearts / she bends down in the decaying light / in the 4th
century / runs her fingers / across the letters / doesn't know
/ exactly / what she sees / in this piece / of wood carved / in
this newly new / language of / *souvenir* / because memory
/ is a kind of grief / desire another / but we see it / the
churches she will / raise and armies / and throngs / who
will trundle / down all the terrible / roads of the future /
to gaze upon / this sign / to stand / where someone stood /
to hold the past / in their hands / a piece of the story / she
lifts the title / from its casket / sits on her divan / her slaves
fan / the air with fronds / with effort / with the moment /
frozen and heavy / outside the window / the day is hot /
with meaning / is painted / with glaze / with veneer / the
sky is pottery / or poetry / picturesque / the way only /
the past can be

# FOUND POEM

In the dream you are at the conference
in the city where the poets congregate
and there is opulence and elegance
and wine the color of golden grass
and you are looking for someone,
a friend, with her mind full of genius
and snakes, and when you find her
after wandering the caravan
and behemoth of the conference,
she finally gives you what you have
been looking for this whole time—
*poetry*—and it's a cold white plate
with grapes like small globes
dusted and going dark and full of juice
and cheese like the aged fruit of the earth,
and you stare at the grapes and the cheese
for a long time so that when you finally
look up, you see that your friend
has vanished into the wild luxury
that spins on around you like a galaxy
and she has taken the grapes and cheese
so, at first, you think that she has taken
the thing you wanted but—no—she has
left you holding the cold white plate.

# HOW WE SURVIVE

The gates of Troy are open.

The invasion begins in the nose and the mouth.

We collected years of stillness.

The virus moves down the respiratory tract.

We gathered a decade of patience.

Hector is dead and that leaves Priam and Hector's son, Astynax,
vulnerable inside the city.

Lung tissue is the primary battle zone, but a fraction of the virus attacks
the kidney. As on the real battlefield, if two places are being attacked at
the same time, each place gets worse.

We farmed tranquility.

The trajectory is an overreaction of the immune system known as a
"cytokine storm."

Aeneas is second only to Hector. He has lived in Troy a long time.

The virus attacks the heart muscle and the blood vessels.

He is a legendary warrior, but he is beaten in battle, twice.

We quarried distance.

The disruption extends to the blood itself.

The Greeks flow into the city with a tempest of fire and swords.

We masked ourselves in barricades.

They find Priam and Astynax alone in the palace.

The gods save Aeneas. Both times.

The cytokine storm causes brain swelling. The blood's exaggerated tendency to clot triggers strokes.

The Greeks spear Priam as he clings to the statue of Apollo and leave his body for the dogs.

Aeneas carries his father on his back.

Again and again, we kept each other.

The Greeks throw Astynax from the walls of the palace.

Aeneas' son walks by his side.

He loves the city. He leaves the city.

Across the wine-dark sea, Aeneas carries his people with him.

# FOUND QUARANTINE ODE
# ON FACEBOOK

Remember when
we all thought
it was sad

that a medieval
cathedral caught
on fire? Ah, what

sweet summer
children we were.

# FOUND POEM IN A LETTER
# FROM A FRIEND IN SPAIN

Tell me anything.
Forgive the brevity,
long the hug.

# THE TALE OF THE NEW JERUSALEM

*A new state of affairs will soon exist . . . there will be no death and no illness . . .*
*You will be safe; nothing will harm you here.*

*—from an ad placed in the paper by a local prophet, Farmington, Maine*

The day she predicted comes
without revelation galloping

down from the sky to remake
the city and all of us in an image

immaculate and pure, and her face
on the bandstand is so full

of amazed dismay at the illness
that remains among us, persistent

as plastic trash plaiting the roadway
to this New Jerusalem, that her voice

almost breaks with sorrow at the absence
of health and perpetual youth,

our small town still uncovered by the glorious
bubble of grace she was so sure was coming

she took out ads in the paper. Instead,
low clouds break as the sun sets

and layered light paints us all
gold as we listen to her

assurance that such grace
is still coming. It blunders down

from above like all the wild horses
of the Lord that threaten

to trample us as we trudge
the roadway to the Damascus

of our fractured lives, she says.
But I say: We will be safe-

ly back home soon, my friend,
don't worry, and the red

in our glasses of wine
will be a color closer to black

and the sky will be a silk bubble
of stars and our conversation

will leave the pandemic
and the City of God. It will move

into other fields plowed
by our ignorance and laughter

will waver up off us like heat
from the pavement in that city,

heat that will eventually consume
us and everything and all

we love—this paradise we are
surprised to learn is already ours.

# HOW IT BURNED: EPILOGUE

*pieces of the true cross, the thorned crown, and nails*
*from the crucifixion were housed in Notre Dame, Paris*

when      the      spire
transformed   into collapse
when wreckage  when the
final architecture of itself
failed when the roof from
rose   window   to   bell
buckled and fell into the
channel of flame and ash
that once was a sanctuary
when the mist of hoses
soaked the faces of those
who watched from the
river   who watched from
the *quai* who held hands
to  comfort  each  other
people put other hands into
the   fire  they  tried  to
save the relics the pieces of
the  cross  the  nail  the
thorns  they burned but so
what if they burned so what
if  they  turned  to  ash    as
Genesis says but of us   so
what if nothing remains of

them but us but no
really what if the hands
reaching          through
flames were just there
to console us

# NOTES AND ACKNOWLEDGMENTS

This book is what it is due to the help, kindness, and blessing of numerous wonderful people. Chad and Greg—thanks for your friendship and even more thanks for inviting me and hosting me in Italy where this tale began. To Christopher, likewise. To Carey, thanks for believing in my work and for the power of your editorial eye, but even more for your kindness and friendship. Thanks to Alyssa and Emily and the whole crew at AJB for all the work you do, nurturing poets and poetry. Thanks to Kristen who read an early version of this book and helped make it better. Christian, Gibson, Matt, and Rob also read many of these poems and made them better, too. Thanks to you guys. Thanks, too, to my colleagues and students at the University of Maine Farmington and beyond who teach me so much every day about what it means to make a life in poetry. Thanks to Julian, again, for coming with me and being the best travel companion a dad could ask for. Thanks to Jennifer Anne for her love and light and for all she brings to my life. And finally, to all the unnamed people who helped me and consoled me through the pandemic: thank you for carrying me.

Thanks, too, to the editors of the following journals and websites for featuring the poems below:

"How it Burned," *Maine Magazine*

"Infinite Jest," *Sojourners*

"Cause and Effect," *America*

"Galileo's Middle Finger," *The Café Review*

"The Tale of the Uncorrupted Body of St. Sebastian of the Carts," *Zocalo: Public Square*

"Found Quarantine Ode on FB," *ROOM: A Sketchbook for Analytic Action*

"MUSA Underwater Sculpture Garden" (as "Underwater Sculpture Garden, Isla Mujeres, Mexico"), *Terrain.org.*

"How it Began" and "How We Survived" were published in *Wait: Poems from the Pandemic,* Littoral Books.

"The Fingers of Doubting Thomas" and "St. Bartholomew Flayed" were featured in the Assisi International Contemporary Arts Exhibition, September 2020, Art Gallery Le Logge, Assisi, Italy.

"The Tale of the Grief Stopper" includes a reference to Agathon's speech in Plato's *Symposium:* Love, Agathon says, "walks not upon the earth, nor yet upon skulls of men, which are not so very soft, but in the hearts and souls of both god, and men, which are of all things the softest . . ."

"Ode to the Stone Spheres" riffs on Yeats' "The Second Coming":

> Things fall apart; the center cannot hold;
> Mere anarchy is loosed upon the world.

"The Tale of the Alphabet" is indebted to Roberto Calasso's book, *The Marriage of Cadmus and Harmony.*

"Two Sheep God" uses information from the first episode of Doug Metzger's podcast, *Literature and History*: www.literatureandhistory.com

"The Well of the Staff" mentions Yeats' poem, "The Wild Swans at Coole":

> The nineteenth autumn has come upon me
> Since I first made my count;
> I saw, before I had well finished,

All suddenly mount
And scatter wheeling in great broken rings
Upon their clamorous wings.

Selections from "How We Survived" and "How We Survive" are from *Science*, *Scripps Research*, and Ellen Bryant Voight's *Kyrie*.

"Poem with the Name of a Costa Rica Beach" is for Drew Barton.

"Found Quarantine Ode on Facebook" is for Dan Salerno.

"Found Poem in a Letter from a Friend in Spain" is for José de María Romero Barea.

# RECENT TITLES FROM ALICE JAMES BOOKS

*Constellation Route*, Matthew Olzmann

*How to Not Be Afraid of Everything*, Jane Wong

*Brocken Spectre*, Jacques J. Rancourt

*No Ruined Stone*, Shara McCallum

*The Vault*, Andrés Cerpa

*White Campion*, Donald Revell

*Last Days*, Tamiko Beyer

*If This Is the Age We End Discovery*, Rosebud Ben-Oni

*Pretty Tripwire*, Alessandra Lynch

Inheritance, Taylor Johnson

*The Voice of Sheila Chandra*, Kazim Ali

*Arrow*, Sumita Chakraborty

*Country, Living*, Ira Sadoff

*Hot with the Bad Things*, Lucia LoTempio

*Witch*, Philip Matthews

*Neck of the Woods*, Amy Woolard

*Little Envelope of Earth Conditions*, Cori A. Winrock

*Aviva-No*, Shimon Adaf, Translated by Yael Segalovitz

*Half/Life: New & Selected Poems*, Jeffrey Thomson

*Odes to Lithium*, Shira Erlichman

*Here All Night*, Jill McDonough

*To the Wren: Collected & New Poems*, Jane Mead

*Angel Bones*, Ilyse Kusnetz

*Monsters I Have Been*, Kenji C. Liu

*Soft Science*, Franny Choi

*Bicycle in a Ransacked City: An Elegy*, Andrés Cerpa

*Anaphora*, Kevin Goodan

*Ghost, like a Place*, Iain Haley Pollock

ALICE JAMES BOOKS is committed to publishing books that matter. The press was founded in 1973 in Boston, Massachusetts as a cooperative, wherein authors performed the day-to-day undertakings of the press. This element remains present today, as authors who publish with the press are invited to collaborate closely in the publication process of their work. AJB remains committed to its founders' original feminist mission, while expanding upon the scope to include all voices and poets who might otherwise go unheard. In keeping with its efforts to build equity and increase inclusivity in publishing and the literary arts, AJB seeks out poets whose writing possesses the range, depth, and ability to cultivate empathy in our world and to dynamically push against silence. The press was named for Alice James, sister to William and Henry, whose extraordinary gift for writing went unrecognized during her lifetime.

*Designed by Alban Fischer*

*Printed by McNaughton & Gunn*